High Fiber Diet Cookbook

Easy And Healthy High Fiber Recipes!

GW00458004

Table of Contents

Introduction

Unfortunately most people do not realize how important fiber is for your diet, and how beneficial it can be for your health. Including high amounts of fiber in your diet can help reduce your risk of serious illnesses like diabetes and cancer. Because fiber digests more slowly in your body, it will make you feel full for longer, and will help you lose weight.

Great Sources of High Fiber Include:

- Beans and lentils
- Brown rice
- Fruits
- Potato skins
- Whole wheat bread
- Flax seed

This cookbook provides high fiber recipes that are healthy and packed with flavors.

Chapter 1: High Fiber Breakfast Recipes

Rhubarb Porridge

Ingredients

1½ cups skim milk

½ cup orange juice

1 cup old-fashioned rolled oats

1 cup ½-inch pieces rhubarb, fresh or frozen

½ teaspoon ground cinnamon

2-3 tablespoons brown sugar

2 tablespoons chopped pecans or other nuts, toasted

Pinch of salt

Directions

Combine milk, juice, oats, rhubarb, cinnamon and salt in a medium saucepan. Bring to a boil over medium-high heat. Reduce heat, cover and cook at a very gentle bubble, stirring frequently, until the oats and rhubarb are tender, about 5 minutes.

Remove from the heat and let stand, covered, for 5 minutes. Stir in sweetener to taste. Top with nuts.

High Fiber Pancakes

Ingredients

2½ cups whole-wheat flour

1 cup buttermilk powder

5 tablespoons dried egg whites

¼ cup sugar

1½ tablespoons baking powder

2 teaspoons baking soda

1 teaspoon salt

1 cup flaxseed meal

1 cup nonfat dry milk

½ cup wheat bran, or oat bran

1½ cups nonfat milk

¼ cup canola oil

1 teaspoon vanilla extract

Directions

Whisk flour, buttermilk powder, dried egg whites, sugar, baking powder, baking soda and salt in a large bowl. Stir in flaxseed meal, dry milk and bran. (Makes 6 cups dry mix.)

Combine milk, oil and vanilla in a glass measuring cup.

Place 2 cups pancake mix in a large bowl. Refrigerate the remaining pancake mix in an airtight container for up to 1 month.

Make a well in the center of the pancake mix. Whisk in the milk mixture until just blended; do not overmix. Let stand for 5 minutes.

Coat a nonstick skillet or griddle with cooking spray and place over medium heat. Whisk the batter. Using ¼ cup batter for each pancake, cook pancakes until the edges are dry and bubbles begin to form, about 2 minutes.

Turnover and cook until golden brown, about 2 minutes longer. Adjust heat as necessary for even browning.

Mango Oatmeal

Ingredients

1/2 cup oats

1/4 cup low-fat milk

1/3 cup low-fat plain yogurt

1/8 teaspoon almond extract

1/2 cup diced mango

1 teaspoon honey

1 teaspoon chia seeds

Directions

Add oats to your container of choice and pour in milk and low-fat yogurt.

Mix in almond extract. Add a layer of mango. Top off with a drizzle of honey and chia seeds.

Oat Date Muffins

Ingredients
1 cup plus 2 tablespoons old-fashioned oats

⅓ cup chopped walnuts

1 cup whole-wheat flour

¾ cup all-purpose flour

⅓ cup whole flaxseeds, ground

2 large eggs

⅔ cup packed light brown sugar

¾ cup buttermilk

½ cup orange juice

¼ cup canola oil

2 tablespoons freshly grated orange zest

1 teaspoon vanilla extract

¾ cup chopped pitted dates

2 teaspoons baking powder

½ teaspoon baking soda

¼ teaspoon salt

Directions
Preheat oven to 400°F. Coat 12 muffin cups with cooking spray.

Spread 1 cup oats and the walnuts, if using, in 2 separate small baking pans. Bake, stirring once or twice, until light golden and fragrant, 4 to 6 minutes for the nuts and 8 to 10 minutes for the oats. Transfer to a plate to cool.

Meanwhile, whisk whole-wheat flour, all-purpose flour, flaxseeds, baking powder, baking soda and salt in a medium bowl.

Whisk eggs and brown sugar in a medium bowl until smooth. Whisk in buttermilk, orange juice, oil, orange zest and vanilla.

Add to the dry ingredients and mix with a rubber spatula just until moistened. Fold in dates, the toasted oats and nuts, if using. Scoop batter into the prepared muffin cups. Sprinkle the tops with the remaining 2 tablespoons oats.

Bake the muffins until the tops are golden brown and spring back when touched lightly, 15 to 25 minutes.

Let cool in the pan for 5 minutes. Loosen edges and turn muffins out onto a wire rack to cool slightly before serving.

Cinnamon Apple Oatmeal

Ingredients

1 cup water

1/4 cup apple juice

1 apple, cored and chopped

2/3 cup rolled oats

1 teaspoon ground cinnamon

1 cup milk

Directions

Combine the water, apple juice, and apples in a saucepan. Bring to a boil over high heat, and stir in the rolled oats and cinnamon.

Return to a boil, then reduce heat to low, and simmer until thick, about 3 minutes. Spoon into serving bowls, and pour milk over the servings.

Banana Breakfast Muffins

Ingredients

2 large eggs

⅔ cup packed light brown sugar

1 cup mashed ripe bananas, (2 medium)

1 cup buttermilk

1 cup unprocessed wheat bran

¾ cup all-purpose flour

1½ teaspoons baking powder

½ teaspoon baking soda

½ teaspoon ground cinnamon

½ cup chocolate chips, (optional)

⅓ cup chopped walnuts

¼ teaspoon salt

¼ cup canola oil

1 teaspoon vanilla extract

1 cup whole-wheat flour

Directions

Preheat oven to 400°F. Coat 12 muffin cups with cooking spray.

Whisk eggs and brown sugar in a medium bowl until smooth. Whisk in bananas, buttermilk, wheat bran, oil and vanilla.

Whisk whole-wheat flour, all-purpose flour, baking powder, baking soda, cinnamon and salt in a large bowl. Make a well in the dry ingredients; add the wet ingredients and stir with a rubber spatula until just combined.

Stir in chocolate chips, if using. Scoop the batter into the prepared muffin cups. Sprinkle with walnuts, if using.

Bake the muffins until the tops are golden brown and spring back when touched lightly, 15 to 25 minutes.

Let cool in the pan for 5 minutes. Loosen edges and turn muffins out onto a wire rack to cool slightly before serving.

Banana Strawberry Muffins

Ingredients

2 eggs

1/2 cup unsweetened applesauce

1/4 cup vegetable oil

3/4 cup packed brown sugar

1 teaspoon vanilla extract

3 bananas, mashed

2 cups whole wheat flour

1 teaspoon baking soda

1 tablespoon ground cinnamon

1 cup frozen sliced strawberries

Directions

Preheat the oven to 375 degrees F (190 degrees C). Grease 12 large muffin cups, or line with paper liners.

In a large bowl, whisk together the eggs, applesauce, oil, brown sugar, vanilla and bananas. Combine the flour, baking soda and cinnamon; Stir into the banana mixture until moistened. Stir in the strawberries until evenly distributed. Spoon batter into muffin cups until completely filled.

Bake for 20 minutes in the preheated oven, or until the tops of the muffins spring back when pressed lightly. Cool before removing from the muffin tins.

Multigrain Cinnamon Pancakes

Ingredients

1/4 cup whole wheat flour

1/4 cup all-purpose flour

1/4 cup rolled oats

1/4 cup cornmeal

2 teaspoons granular sucralose sweetener

1/2 teaspoon salt

1 teaspoon baking powder

1/2 teaspoon baking soda

1/2 teaspoon ground cinnamon

2 egg whites

2 tablespoons plain nonfat yogurt

2 tablespoons skim milk

2 tablespoons water

Directions

In a medium bowl, stir together the whole wheat flour, all-purpose flour, oats, cornmeal, sweetener, salt, baking powder, baking soda and cinnamon. In a separate bowl, whisk together the eggs, yogurt, milk and water. Pour the wet ingredients into the dry, and mix just until moistened.

Heat a skillet over medium heat, and coat with cooking spray. Pour about 1/3 cup of batter per pancake onto the skillet.

Cook until bubbles begin to form in the center, then flip and cook until browned on the other side.

Banana Chocolate Bread

Ingredients

1/3 cup skim milk

1 teaspoon lemon juice

1 3/4 cups whole wheat flour

1/2 cup unsweetened cocoa powder

2 teaspoons baking powder

1/2 teaspoon baking soda

1 teaspoon ground cinnamon

1 teaspoon ground nutmeg

1/2 teaspoon salt

2 large eggs

3/4 cup white sugar

3 ripe bananas, mashed

1 tablespoon canola oil

1 teaspoon vanilla extract

Directions

Preheat oven to 375 F (190 degrees C). Lightly spray a 9x5 inch loaf pan or 16 muffin cups with cooking spray. Stir the skim milk and lemon juice together in a glass measuring cup; let stand until curdled, about 30 minutes. Whisk together the whole wheat flour, cocoa powder, baking powder, baking soda, cinnamon, nutmeg, and salt; set aside.

Beat the eggs and sugar together with an electric mixer until smooth. Mix in the mashed bananas, the milk mixture, canola oil, and vanilla extract. Stir in the flour mixture just until all ingredients are moistened. Pour the batter into the prepared pan or muffin cups.

Bake in the preheated oven until a toothpick inserted into the center comes out clean, about 1 hour for a loaf, or 30 minutes for muffins. Cool in the pan for 10 minutes before removing to cool completely on a wire rack.

Pecan Blueberry Oatmeal

Ingredients

½ cup old-fashioned rolled oats

½ cup water

½ cup blueberries, fresh or frozen, thawed

2 tablespoons nonfat plain Greek yogurt

1 tablespoon toasted chopped pecans

2 teaspoons pure maple syrup

Pinch of salt

Directions

Combine oats, water and salt in a pot. Heat on stove until porridge is cooked, and top with blueberries, yogurt, pecans and syrup.

Whole Grain Buttermilk Pancakes

Ingredients

1/2 cup wheat germ

2 cups whole wheat flour

1 teaspoon baking soda

1/2 teaspoon salt

3 cups buttermilk

2 eggs, lightly beaten

1 tablespoon canola oil

Cooking spray

Directions

Preheat oven to 350 degrees F (175 degrees C).

Spread wheat germ over a baking sheet.

Bake in the preheated oven until toasted, about 5 minutes. Cool slightly, then transfer wheat germ to a large bowl.

Stir flour, baking soda, and salt into wheat germ. Beat buttermilk, eggs, and oil in another bowl until smooth; pour egg mixture into flour mixture and stir until batter is just blended.

Heat griddle over medium-high heat and coat with cooking spray. Pour 1/4 cup portions of batter onto the griddle and cook until bubbles form and the edges are dry, about 2 minutes.

Flip and cook until browned on the other side, about 3 minutes more. Repeat with remaining batter.

Lemon Quinoa Porridge

Ingredients

1 cup quinoa

2 cups nonfat milk

1 pinch salt

3 tablespoons maple syrup

1/2 lemon, zested

1 cup blueberries

2 teaspoons flax seed

Directions

Rinse quinoa in a fine strainer with cold water to remove bitterness until water runs clear and is no longer frothy.

Heat milk in a saucepan over medium heat until warm, 2 to 3 minutes. Stir quinoa and salt into the milk; simmer over medium-low heat until much of the liquid has been absorbed, about 20 minutes.

Remove saucepan from heat. Stir maple syrup and lemon zest into the quinoa mixture. Gently fold blueberries into the mixture.

Divide quinoa mixture between 2 bowls; top each with 1 teaspoon flax seed to serve.

Apple Muffins

Ingredients

2 cups whole wheat flour

1 tablespoon baking powder

1/2 teaspoon salt

1 teaspoon ground cinnamon

3/4 cup nonfat milk

2 egg whites

1/4 cup vegetable oil

1/4 cup honey

1 cup chopped apples

Directions

Preheat oven to 375 degrees F (190 degrees C). Lightly grease one 12-cup muffin tin.

Lightly beat egg whites. In a separate bowl mix dry ingredients thoroughly.

In a separate bowl, mix remaining ingredients. Gently fold in egg white. Add to the dry ingredients. Stir until barely moistened. Batter will be lumpy.

Fill greased muffin tins two-thirds full. Bake about 20 minutes until lightly browned.

Whole Wheat Blueberry Muffins

Ingredients

2 cups whole wheat flour

1/3 cup brown sugar

1/2 teaspoon ground cinnamon

2 teaspoons baking powder

1 teaspoon baking soda

1 1/2 cups mashed bananas

4 egg whites

1 teaspoon vanilla extract

1 cup fresh blueberries

Directions

Preheat oven to 350 degrees F (175 degrees C). Lightly grease a 12 cup muffin pan.

In a large bowl, mix the whole wheat flour, brown sugar, cinnamon, baking powder, and baking soda. In a separate bowl, mix the bananas, egg whites, and vanilla extract.

Mix the banana mixture into the flour mixture until smooth. Fold in the blueberries. Spoon the batter into the prepared muffin pan.

Bake 16 minutes in the preheated oven, or until a toothpick inserted in the center of a muffin comes out clean.

Coconut Oatmeal

Ingredients

3 1/2 cups plain or vanilla soy milk

1/4 teaspoon salt

2 cups rolled oats

1/4 cup pure maple syrup

1/3 cup raisins

1/3 cup dried cranberries

1/3 cup sweetened flaked coconut

1/3 cup chopped walnuts

1 (8 ounce) container plain yogurt (optional)

3 tablespoons honey

Directions

Pour the milk and salt into a saucepan, and bring to a boil. Stir in the oats, maple syrup, raisins, and cranberries. Return to a boil, then reduce heat to medium.

Cook for 5 minutes. Stir in walnuts and coconut, and let stand until it reaches your desired thickness.

Spoon into serving bowls, and top with yogurt and honey, if desired.

Chapter 2: High Fiber Lunch And Salad Recipes

Chicken Quesadillas

Ingredients

4 boneless, skinless chicken breasts, each 4 ounces

1 cup chopped onions

1/2 cup smoky or hot salsa

1 cup chopped fresh tomatoes

1 cup chopped fresh cilantro

6 whole-wheat tortillas, each 8 inches in diameter

1 cup shredded reduced-fat cheddar cheese

Directions

Heat oven to 425 F. Lightly coat a baking sheet with cooking spray.

Cut each chicken breast into cubes. In a large, nonstick frying pan, add the chicken and onions and saute until the onions are tender and the chicken is thoroughly cooked, about 5 to 7 minutes. Remove from heat. Stir in the salsa, tomatoes and cilantro.

To assemble, lay a tortilla flat and rub the outside edge with water. Spread about 1/2 cup of the chicken mixture onto the tortilla, leaving about 1/2 inch free around the outer rim. Sprinkle with a spoonful of shredded cheese. Fold tortilla in half and seal. Place on a cookie sheet. Repeat with the remaining tortillas.

Lightly coat the top of the tortillas with cooking spray. Bake until the quesadillas are lightly browned and crispy, about 5 to 7 minutes. Cut in half and serve immediately.

Bean And Vegetable Quesadillas

Ingredients

1 1/2 cups reduced sodium black beans, drained and rinsed

1 cup finely diced zucchini

1 cup frozen sweet corn kernels, thawed

2/3 cup finely diced red onion

1/2 cup shredded 2% sharp cheddar cheese

1/4 cup chopped fresh cilantro

1 teaspoon cumin

1/2 teaspoon salt

Pinch of black pepper

1/4 teaspoon Tabasco sauce

2 whole-wheat tortillas, 12 inches in diameter

Directions

Heat oven to 350 F. In a large bowl, combine the beans, zucchini, corn, red onion, cheese, cilantro, cumin, salt, pepper and Tabasco sauce.

Heat a large, nonstick skillet to medium heat and coat with cooking spray. Place one tortilla in the pan to warm. Place half the bean mixture on one side of the tortilla and fold over to cover.

Cook for 1 to 2 minutes then flip the quesadilla and cook for another 1 to 2 minutes. Remove from heat and place on a baking sheet. Repeat with the other tortilla.

Bake for 5 to 8 minutes or until cheese has completely melted. Cut each quesadilla into 4 even slices and serve with your choice of condiments.

Tuna And Bean Salad

Ingredients

1/2 whole-grain baguette, torn into 2-inch pieces

3 tablespoons olive oil

1 16-ounce can cannellini beans, drained and rinsed

2 small dill pickles, cut into bite-size pieces

1 small red onion, thinly sliced

2 tablespoons red wine vinegar

1/4 teaspoon pepper

7-ounce pouch tuna, no salt added, drained and rinsed

2 tablespoons finely chopped fresh parsley

Directions

Preheat broiler. Place the baguette pieces on a heavy cookie sheet and brush with 1 tablespoon of the oil.

Place under broiler for about 1 to 2 minutes, until golden. Turn the bread pieces and broil for an additional 1 or 2 minutes.

In a large bowl, combine the remaining oil, beans, pickles, onion, vinegar and pepper. Fold in the broiled baguette pieces.

Divide the mixture among four bowls and top with the tuna and parsley.

Southwest Chicken And Bean Stew

Ingredients

1 lb boneless, skinless chicken breast, diced

1 package reduced-sodium taco seasoning mix

1 15-ounce can unsalted black beans, rinsed under running water and drained

1 1/2 cups frozen corn

3/4 cup fresh or frozen pepper stir-fry vegetables (onions and green, red and yellow peppers), chopped

3/4 cup water

3/4 cup reduced-fat shredded cheddar cheese

Directions

Spray a 10-inch skillet with cooking spray. Add chicken to the skillet; cook over medium-high heat for 2 minutes. Stir occasionally.

Add the seasoning mix, beans, corn, stir-fry mix and water. Cook over medium-high heat for 8 to 10 minutes. Stir frequently until the sauce is slightly thickened and the chicken is no longer pink.

Top with cheese and serve.

Mediterranean Quinoa Salad

Ingredients

1 cup quinoa

1 1/4 cups water

1 lemon, juiced (about 2 tablespoons)

1 garlic clove, minced

1/4 teaspoon ground black pepper

2 tablespoons olive or canola oil

1 large cucumber, seeded and cut into 1/2-inch pieces

1 pint cherry tomatoes, halved

1/3 cup chopped parsley

1/4 cup chopped red onion

1/2 cup reduced-fat feta cheese

Directions

In a medium saucepan over high heat, bring quinoa and water to a boil. Reduce heat to medium-low and cover. Simmer for about 10 minutes or until the quinoa is tender.

Remove quinoa from heat and let stand, covered, for 5 minutes. Then fluff quinoa with a fork and spread it out onto a large rimmed baking sheet to cool.

In a small bowl, whisk lemon juice, garlic and pepper. Gradually whisk in oil.

After the quinoa has cooled, transfer it to a large bowl and add the dressing, cucumber, tomatoes, parsley and onion. Top with feta cheese and toss gently to mix.

Olive Lentil Salad

Ingredients

4 cups water

salt

1 1/4 cups dry lentils

2 large cloves garlic, minced

2 large roma (plum) tomatoes, seeded and chopped

1/2 cup chopped red onion

1/2 cup chopped green bell pepper

1 small green chile pepper, seeded and chopped

1 lemon, juiced

1 teaspoon lemon zest

1 small carrot, shredded

1/2 cup oil-cured black olives

1/4 cup chopped fresh cilantro

salt and ground black pepper to taste

1/4 cup extra-virgin olive oil

2 hard-cooked eggs, cut in half lengthwise

Directions

Bring the water and salt to a boil in a saucepan over high heat. Pour the lentils into the water while stirring constantly. Reduce heat to low, cover, and simmer until the lentils are tender but still hold their shape, about 30 minutes. Drain well.

Transfer the lentils to a mixing bowl and stir in the garlic, seeded tomatoes, red onion, green bell pepper, and chile pepper. Add the juice of 1 lemon plus 1 teaspoon of the zest. Mix in the shredded carrot, olives, and cilantro.

Season with salt and black pepper, and drizzle with olive oil; mix well. Refrigerate for at least an hour to allow the flavors to blend.

Before serving, mix the salad again and add more lemon juice or olive oil if needed. Transfer to a serving dish and garnish with sliced eggs.

Couscous Salad

Ingredients

10 ounces uncooked couscous

2 tablespoons olive oil

1/2 cup lemon juice

3/4 teaspoon salt

1/4 teaspoon ground black pepper

1 cucumber, seeded and chopped

1/2 cup finely chopped green onions

1/2 cup fresh parsley, chopped

1/4 cup fresh basil, chopped

6 leaves lettuce

6 slices lemon

Directions

In a medium saucepan, bring 1 3/4 cup water to a boil. Stir in couscous; cover. Remove from heat; let stand, covered, 5 minutes. Cool to room temperature.

Meanwhile, in a medium bowl combine oil, lemon juice, salt and pepper. Stir in cucumber, green onion, parsley, basil and couscous. Mix well and chill for at least 1 hour.

Line a plate with lettuce leaves. Spoon couscous mixture over leaves and garnish with lemon wedges.

Mediterranean Bean Salad

Ingredients

1 (15 ounce) can cannellini (white kidney) beans, rinsed and drained

1 (15 ounce) can garbanzo beans, rinsed and drained

1 (15 ounce) can dark red kidney beans, rinsed and drained

1/2 onion, minced

2 cloves garlic, minced

2 tablespoons minced fresh parsley, or to taste

1/4 cup olive oil

1 lemon, juiced

salt and ground black pepper to taste

Directions

Combine cannellini beans, garbanzo beans, kidney beans in a mixing bowl. Add onion, garlic, parsley, olive oil, lemon juice, salt, and black pepper; mix well.

Cilantro Quinoa Salad

Ingredients

1 1/2 cups water

1 cup uncooked quinoa, rinsed

1/4 cup red bell pepper, chopped

1/4 cup yellow bell pepper, chopped

1 small red onion, finely chopped

1 1/2 teaspoons curry powder

1/4 cup chopped fresh cilantro

1 lime, juiced

1/4 cup toasted sliced almonds

1/2 cup minced carrots

1/2 cup dried cranberries

salt and ground black pepper to taste

Directions

Pour the water into a saucepan, and cover with a lid. Bring to a boil over high heat, then pour in the quinoa, recover, and continue to simmer over low heat until the water has been absorbed, 15 to 20 minutes.

Scrape into a mixing bowl, and chill in the refrigerator until cold.

Once cold, stir in the red bell pepper, yellow bell pepper, red onion, curry powder, cilantro, lime juice, sliced almonds, carrots, and cranberries.

Season to taste with salt and pepper. Chill before serving.

Spinach Berry Salad

Ingredients

6 cups fresh spinach, torn into bite-size pieces

1 cup thickly sliced strawberries

1 cup blueberries, trimmed

1 small red onion, thinly sliced

1/2 cup chopped pecans

Non-Fat Curry Dressing:

2 tablespoons balsamic vinegar

2 tablespoons rice vinegar

4 teaspoons honey

1 teaspoon curry powder

2 teaspoons Dijon mustard

1 pinch Salt and pepper to taste

Directions

Wash and dry spinach. Whip together dressing ingredients. Add to spinach and toss lightly. Add berries, onion and pecans. Toss lightly and serve.

Chickpea Mediterranean Salad

Ingredients

1 (15 ounce) can garbanzo beans (chickpeas), drained and rinsed

1 roma (plum) tomato, seeded and diced

1/2 medium green bell pepper, diced

1 small onion, finely chopped

1 small clove garlic, minced

1 tablespoon chopped fresh parsley

2 tablespoons olive oil

1 lemon, juiced

Directions

In a bowl, toss together the garbanzo beans, roma tomato, green bell pepper, onion, garlic, parsley, olive oil, and lemon juice. Cover, and chill until serving.

Basil Quinoa Salad

Ingredients

2 cups low-sodium chicken broth

1 cup quinoa

1 large lemon, zested and juiced

1/2 cup roasted red peppers, drained and diced

1/4 cup dried cranberries

2 tablespoons minced red onion

2 tablespoons chopped fresh basil

Directions

Bring chicken broth and quinoa to a boil in a saucepan. Reduce heat to medium-low, cover, and simmer until quinoa is tender and broth has been absorbed, 15 to 20 minutes.

Stir quinoa, lemon zest, and lemon juice together in a bowl. Add red peppers, cranberries, onion, and basil to quinoa; toss to combine.

Black Bean Salsa Soup

Ingredients

2 (15 ounce) cans black beans, drained and rinsed

1 1/2 cups vegetable broth

1 cup chunky salsa

1 teaspoon ground cumin

4 tablespoons sour cream

2 tablespoons thinly sliced green onion

Directions

In an electric food processor or blender, combine beans, broth, salsa, and cumin. Blend until fairly smooth.

Heat the bean mixture in a saucepan over medium heat until thoroughly heated.

Ladle soup into 4 individual bowls, and top each bowl with 1 tablespoon of the sour cream and 1/2 tablespoon green onion.

Brown Rice Salad

Ingredients

1 cup uncooked brown rice

1 1/2 cups water

1 (15 ounce) can kidney beans, rinsed and drained

1/4 cup chopped red onion

1/4 cup sliced fresh mushrooms

1/4 cup bite-size broccoli florets

1/4 cup chopped green bell pepper

1/4 cup chopped red bell pepper

1/4 cup chopped yellow bell pepper

2 tablespoons chopped raw almonds

1/4 teaspoon coarse black pepper

2 tablespoons fat free Italian-style dressing

1 tablespoon extra-virgin olive oil

Directions

Combine the rice and water in a small saucepan; bring to a boil over high heat. Cover, and reduce the heat to medium-low. Simmer until the rice is tender, and the liquid has been absorbed, 45 to 50 minutes. Remove from heat and allow to cool.

Place cooled rice in a large bowl. Stir in the kidney beans, red onions, mushrooms, broccoli, bell peppers, and almonds; season with pepper. Toss salad with the Italian dressing and olive oil.

Chill for at least one hour before serving.

Chapter 3: High Fiber Main Dish Recipes

Chicken Bean Chili

Ingredients

1 tablespoon olive oil

4 skinless, boneless chicken breast halves - cubed

1 onion, chopped

1 1/4 cups chicken broth

1 (4 ounce) can diced green chiles

1 teaspoon garlic powder

1 teaspoon ground cumin

1/2 teaspoon dried oregano

1/2 teaspoon dried cilantro

1/8 teaspoon cayenne pepper

1 (15 ounce) can cannellini beans, drained and rinsed

2 green onions, chopped

2 ounces shredded Monterey Jack cheese

Directions

Heat oil in a large saucepan over medium-high heat. Cook chicken and onion in oil 4 to 5 minutes, or until onion is tender.

Stir in the chicken broth, green chiles, garlic powder, cumin, oregano, cilantro, and cayenne pepper. Reduce heat, and simmer for 15 minutes.

Stir in the beans, and simmer for 5 more minutes, or until chicken is no longer pink and juices run clear. Garnish with green onion and shredded cheese.

Chicken Pasta Casserole

Ingredients

12 ounces whole-wheat pasta

16 mini sweet peppers

1½ pounds boneless, skinless chicken breast, cut into ¾-inch pieces

3 tablespoons extra-virgin olive oil, divided

1 teaspoon salt, divided

½ teaspoon ground pepper

2 medium fennel bulbs, chopped, plus ¼ cup chopped fronds

⅓ cup finely chopped shallot

3 tablespoons all-purpose flour

1½ cups low-sodium chicken broth

½ cup dry white wine

½ cup crème fraîche

½ cup chopped fresh chives, divided

2 tablespoons lemon juice

½ cup olives, chopped

½ cup whole wheat breadcrumbs

Directions

Bring a large pot of water to a boil. Cook pasta according to package directions. Drain and transfer to a large bowl. Set aside.

Position a rack in upper third of oven; preheat broiler to high. Line a rimmed baking sheet with foil. Coat the foil with cooking spray.

Place peppers on one side of the prepared baking sheet. Toss chicken, 1 tablespoon oil, ½ teaspoon salt and pepper in a medium bowl. Place the chicken in an even layer on the other half of the baking sheet. Broil, turning once, until the peppers start to char on both sides and the chicken is no longer pink in the middle, 4 to 8 minutes. Set aside to cool slightly.

Preheat oven to 400°F.

Meanwhile, heat 1 tablespoon oil in a large skillet over medium heat. Add fennel and shallot and cook, stirring frequently, until softened and starting to brown, about 5 minutes. Add flour and stir to coat. Add broth and wine and bring to a simmer. Cook, stirring occasionally, until slightly thickened, about 2 minutes. Remove from heat. Stir in crème fraîche, ¼ cup chives, lemon juice, the fennel fronds and the remaining ½ teaspoon salt. Transfer to the bowl with the pasta.

Trim and quarter the peppers. Add the peppers, chicken and olives to the pasta; stir to combine. Transfer the mixture to a 9-by-13-inch casserole dish. Combine bread crumbs with the remaining 1 tablespoon oil in a small bowl. Sprinkle over the casserole.

Bake the casserole until hot, about 30 minutes. Serve topped with the remaining ¼ cup chives.

Brown Rice Chicken Soup

Ingredients

5 cups chicken broth

2 skinless, boneless chicken breast halves

1 cup diced celery

1 cup diced onion

1/4 cup diced carrots

1/4 cup corn

1/4 cup drained and rinsed black beans

1 teaspoon dried sage

1 teaspoon ground black pepper

1 teaspoon salt

1 bay leaf

3/4 cup brown rice

Directions

Bring chicken broth to a boil in a large pot; cook chicken breasts in the boiling water until no longer pink in the center, about 20 minutes. Remove chicken from the chicken broth using a slotted spoon and shred with a fork.

Stir shredded chicken, celery, onion, carrots, corn, black beans, sage, pepper, salt, and bay leaves into the chicken broth and cook until vegetables are slightly softened and flavors of soup have blended, about 20 minutes.

Add brown rice to soup and simmer until rice is tender, about 1 hour.

Cheesy Black Bean Casserole

Ingredients

1/3 cup brown rice

1 cup vegetable broth

1 tablespoon olive oil

1/3 cup diced onion

1 medium zucchini, thinly sliced

2 cooked skinless boneless chicken breast halves, chopped

1/2 cup sliced mushrooms

1/2 teaspoon cumin

salt to taste

ground cayenne pepper to taste

1 (15 ounce) can black beans, drained

1 (4 ounce) can diced green chile peppers, drained

1/3 cup shredded carrots

2 cups shredded Swiss cheese

Directions

Mix the rice and vegetable broth in a pot, and bring to a boil. Reduce heat to low, cover, and simmer 45 minutes, or until rice is tender.

Preheat oven to 350 degrees F (175 degrees C). Lightly grease a large casserole dish.

Heat the olive oil in a skillet over medium heat, and cook the onion until tender. Mix in the zucchini, chicken, and mushrooms. Season with cumin, salt, and ground cayenne pepper. Cook and stir until zucchini is lightly browned and chicken is heated through.

In large bowl, mix the cooked rice, onion, zucchini, chicken, mushrooms, beans, chiles, carrots, and 1/2 the Swiss cheese. Transfer to the prepared casserole dish, and sprinkle with remaining cheese.

Cover casserole loosely with foil, and bake 30 minutes in the preheated oven. Uncover, and continue baking 10 minutes, or until bubbly and lightly browned.

Chicken Barley Casserole

Ingredients

1 chicken breast (cooked)

4 slices bacon, fat removed and meat finely chopped

1 onion, thinly sliced

2 carrots, diced

12 button mushrooms, quartered

2 1/2 cups chicken stock

1 cup barley

1 teaspoon dried thyme

1 teaspoon dried marjoram

1 teaspoon dried parsley

1 bay leaf, crushed

ground black pepper to taste

1 green bell pepper, chopped

Directions

Preheat oven to 375 degrees F (190 degrees C).

In a large skillet, fry bacon until browned. Add onions and carrots to skillet and saute 2 minutes. Add mushrooms, stock, barley, thyme, marjoram, parsley, bay leaf and pepper to taste. Mix all together and spread mixture in a 9x13 inch baking dish. Add green bell pepper on top and stir to settle.

Chop chicken breast and place chicken on top of barley mixture, cover baking dish and bake in the preheated oven for 1 hour and 10 minutes.

Spinach and Barley Stew

Ingredients

1 cup uncooked pearl barley

3 cups water

1 teaspoon olive oil

1 cup chopped yellow onion

2 cloves garlic, minced

1/2 teaspoon dried rosemary

3/4 cup small fresh mushrooms

1 cup chopped yellow bell pepper

2 tablespoons white wine

1 (15.5 ounce) can white beans, drained and rinsed

1 (14.5 ounce) can Italian-style diced tomatoes, drained

2 cups fresh spinach

1 pinch red pepper flakes

Directions

Bring the barley and water to a boil in a pot. Cover, reduce heat to low, and simmer 30 minutes, or until tender.

Heat the olive oil in a large pot over medium heat, and cook the onion and garlic until tender. Season with rosemary. Mix the mushrooms, yellow bell pepper, and wine into the pot, and cook 5 minutes.

Stir in the cooked barley, beans, tomatoes, and spinach. Season with red pepper flakes. Continue cooking 10 minutes, or until spinach is wilted.

Chicken Enchilada Casserole

Ingredients

1½ cups water

¾ cup quinoa

1 tablespoon extra-virgin olive oil

2 medium poblano peppers, chopped

1 jalapeño pepper, finely chopped

½ medium onion, chopped

1 tablespoon chili powder

2 teaspoons ground cumin

½ teaspoon salt

2½ cups shredded or cubed cooked chicken

1 (15 ounce) can green or red enchilada sauce, divided

¾ cup shredded Monterey Jack cheese, divided

Chopped tomato, avocado, scallion and or cilantro for garnish

Directions

Preheat oven to 350°F. Coat an 8-inch-square baking dish with cooking spray.

Combine water and quinoa in a medium saucepan. Bring to a boil. Reduce heat, cover and cook until the water is absorbed and the quinoa is tender, about 15 minutes. Remove from heat and fluff with a fork.

Meanwhile, heat oil in a large skillet over medium heat. Add poblanos, jalapeno, onion, chili powder, cumin and salt. Cook, stirring, until the vegetables are softened and starting to brown, about 5 minutes. Add chicken and ¾ cup enchilada sauce and cook, stirring, until heated through, 2 to 3 minutes. Remove from heat.

Spread half of the cooked quinoa in the prepared baking dish. Sprinkle with half the cheese and top with the chicken mixture. Spread the remaining quinoa on top of the filling. Drizzle the remaining enchilada sauce on top and sprinkle with the remaining cheese.

Bake until the casserole is hot and the cheese is melted, 25 to 30 minutes. Serve topped with tomato, avocado, scallion and/or cilantro, if desired.

Vegetable Barley Soup

Ingredients

2 quarts vegetable broth

1 cup uncooked barley

2 large carrots, chopped

2 stalks celery, chopped

1 (14.5 ounce) can diced tomatoes with juice

1 zucchini, chopped

1 (15 ounce) can garbanzo beans, drained

1 onion, chopped

3 bay leaves

1 teaspoon garlic powder

1 teaspoon white sugar

1 teaspoon salt

1/2 teaspoon ground black pepper

1 teaspoon dried parsley

1 teaspoon curry powder

1 teaspoon paprika

1 teaspoon Worcestershire sauce

Directions

Pour the vegetable broth into a large pot. Add the barley, carrots, celery, tomatoes, zucchini, garbanzo beans, onion, and bay leaves.

Season with garlic powder, sugar, salt, pepper, parsley, curry powder, paprika, and Worcestershire sauce.

Bring to a boil, then cover and simmer over medium-low heat for 90 minutes. The soup will be very thick. You may adjust by adding more broth or less barley if desired.

Remove bay leaves before serving.

Brown Rice And Chicken Stir Fry

Ingredients

2 tablespoons vegetable oil, divided

8 ounces skinless, boneless chicken breast, cut into strips

1/2 red bell pepper, chopped

1/2 cup green onion, chopped

4 cloves garlic, minced

3 cups cooked brown rice

2 tablespoons light soy sauce

1 tablespoon rice vinegar

1 cup frozen peas, thawed

Directions

Heat 1 tablespoon of vegetable oil in a large skillet set over medium heat. Add the chicken, bell pepper, green onion and garlic. Cook and stir until the chicken is cooked through, about 5 minutes. Remove the chicken to a plate and keep warm.

Heat the remaining tablespoon of oil in the same skillet over medium-high heat. Add the rice; cook and stir to heat through. Stir in the soy sauce, rice vinegar and peas, and continue to cook for 1 minute.

Return the chicken mixture to the skillet and stir to blend with the rice and heat through before serving.

Turkey Rice Casserole

Ingredients

1½ cups long-grain brown rice

3 cups reduced-sodium chicken broth

4 cups diced zucchini , and/or summer squash (about 1 pound)

2 red or green bell peppers, chopped

1 large onion, diced

¾ teaspoon salt

1½ cups low-fat milk

3 tablespoons all-purpose flour

2 cups shredded pepper Jack cheese, divided

1 cup fresh or frozen (thawed) corn kernels

2 teaspoons extra-virgin olive oil

8 ounces turkey sausage, casings removed

4 ounces reduced-fat cream cheese

¼ cup chopped pickled jalapeños

Directions

Preheat oven to 375°F.

Pour rice into a 9-by-13-inch baking dish. Bring broth to a simmer in a small saucepan. Stir hot broth into the rice along with zucchini (and/or squash), bell peppers, onion and salt. Cover with foil. Bake for 45 minutes. Remove foil and continue baking until the rice is tender and most of the liquid is absorbed, 35 to 45 minutes more.

Meanwhile, whisk milk and flour in a small saucepan. Cook over medium heat until bubbling and thickened, 3 to 4 minutes. Reduce heat to low. Add 1½ cups Jack cheese and corn and cook, stirring, until the cheese is melted. Set aside.

Heat oil in a large skillet over medium heat and add sausage. Cook, stirring and breaking the sausage into small pieces with a spoon, until lightly browned and no longer pink, about 4 minutes.

When the rice is done, stir in the sausage and cheese sauce. Sprinkle the remaining ½ cup Jack cheese on top and dollop cream cheese by the teaspoonful over the casserole. Top with jalapenos.

Return the casserole to the oven and bake until the cheese is melted, about 10 minutes. Let stand for about 10 minutes before serving.

Vegetable Fried Rice Stir Fry

Ingredients

2 tablespoons rice vinegar

1 teaspoon toasted sesame oil

Hot red pepper sauce, to taste

1 cup instant brown rice

1 cup vegetable broth

2 eggs, lightly beaten

2 teaspoons canola oil

1 clove garlic, minced

1 medium red bell pepper, thinly sliced into 1-inch pieces

4 scallions, cut into 1-inch pieces

4 teaspoons reduced-sodium soy sauce

1 tablespoon minced fresh ginger

6 ounces asparagus spears, trimmed and cut into 1-inch pieces

Directions

Combine rice and broth in a small saucepan. Bring to a boil over high heat. Cover, reduce heat and simmer until the liquid is absorbed, 12 to 14 minutes. Spread the rice out on a large plate and let stand for 5 minutes.

While the rice is cooling, coat a large nonstick wok or skillet with cooking spray and place over medium heat. Pour in eggs and cook, stirring gently, until just set, 30 seconds to 1 minute. Transfer to a small bowl.

Heat canola oil in the pan over medium-high; add asparagus and cook, stirring, for 2 minutes. Add bell pepper, scallions, garlic and ginger; cook, stirring, until the vegetables are just tender, about 2 minutes.

Add the cooked rice, soy sauce and vinegar to the pan; cook until the liquid is absorbed, 30 seconds to 1 minute.

Fold in the cooked eggs. Remove from the heat; stir in sesame oil and hot sauce.

Printed in Great Britain
by Amazon

29641326R00040